Warriors
of the Medieval World

Warriors
of the Medieval World

PAULA HAMMOND

amber
BOOKS

Published by
Amber Books Ltd
74–77 White Lion Street
London
N1 9PF
United Kingdom
www.amberbooks.co.uk
Appstore: itunes.com/apps/amberbooksltd
Facebook: www.facebook.com/amberbooks
Twitter: @amberbooks

ISBN: 978-1-78274-447-4

Project Editor: Michael Spilling
Designer: Zoe Mellors
Picture Research: Terry Forshaw

Printed in China

Picture Credits

AKG Images: 16/17 (Giuseppe Rava), 22/23 (Album/Oronoz), 43 (Pictures From History), 45 (Album/Oronoz), 53 (Pictures From History), 103 (Erich Lessing), 104/105, 110 (British Library)

Alamy: 1 (Jeremy Sutton-Hibbert), 7 (Choups), 10 (Ben Molyneux), 14/15 (Tom Lovell/National Geographic), 20/21 (A.F. Archive), 32/33 (Christopher Ison), 35 (HIP), 36 (Karl Johaentges), 36b (Holmes Garden Photos), 37 (North Wind), 39 (Fine Art Images), 40/41 (VPC Travel Photo), 41 (Fine Art Images), 44 (Interfoto), 46/47 (Pauline Taylor), 49 (Photos 12), 50/51 (Choups), 54/55 (Ancient Art & Architecture Collection), 60t (World History Archive), 69 (Conrad Elias), 70 (Doug Steley B), 70/71 (ITAR-TASS), 74/75 (EPA), 76/77 (HIP), 80/81 (Photos 12), 82/83 (Peter Horree), 84t (Tim Gainey), 84/85 (Jody Fairish), 86 (Detail Heritage), 87 (Photos 12), 90 (Photos 12), 91b (Holmes Garden Photos), 94/95 (Charles Stirling), 95 (Detail Heritage), 96/97 (Vova Pomortzeff), 97 (Skipping Cricket), 100/101 (Mark Sisson), 108/109 (A.F. Archive), 111 (GL Archive), 114 (Hemis), 115 (Hemis), 120/121 (A.F. Archive), 123b (Zoonar) 124/125 (Image Broker)

Amber Books: 6/7, 24/25, 56/57, 78/79, 98/99, 116/117, 122b, 123t

Bridgeman Art Library: 47 (Biblioteque Nationale)

Corbis: 64 (Mike Raabe)

Creative Commons: 60b (Rama CC by S.A. 2.0 Fr)

Depositphotos: 8 (Nejron), 17 (Andrey Kuzmin), 26 (Sergii Figurnyi), 27 (Andreii Chernov), 29bl (Mike Aubry), 30 (Friday), 31 (Elena Yakusheva), 38r (Nigel Spooner), 52 (Rawpixel), 72/73 (Dimaberkut), 84b (Luis Angel Garcia), 92 (Ensuper)

Dorling Kindersley: 13 all, 63, 66t, 67

Dreamstime: 9 (Laurie Barr), 11b (Jorisvo), 12 (Aleksandar Todorovic), 28 (HP Photo), 29t (Vasilly Koval), 34/35 (Anna Yakimova), 68 (Andre Nantel), 88/89 (Vadimmus), 91t (Jarihin), 102/103 (Freesurf 69), 106 (Christian Delbert)

Fotolia: 11t (Thomas Owen)

Getty Images: 18/19 (Gill Yaari/NurPhoto), 42 (John & Lisa Merrill), 62/63 (Matej Divizna), 66r (De Agostini), 93 (Matej Divizna), 122t (De Agostini)

Paula Hammond: 38l, 65, 66b, 107

Library of Congress: 58/59, 59, 61

Mary Evans Picture Library/Historic England: 112, 113, 118/119

Photos.com: 29br, 48l, 68 all except top

Traditionalbowshop.com: 48r

CONTENTS

THE MEDIEVAL WORLD

The Medieval period dates from the fall of the Roman Empire in the fifth century CE, to the 15th century. Europe became a Christian continent, while Islam rose in the Middle East and conquered many lands in North Africa and Southern Europe.
During the Crusades (1096-1487) Western European Christians tried to regain control of the Holy Land from Muslim rulers.

Above: Mongol cavalry armies swept across Asia and into Eastern Europe during the 13th century, conquering all before them.

Left: The battles mentioned in the book are marked on the map.

CHAPTER 1

KNIGHTS AND ARMOUR

Thundering hooves. The clash of metals. The smell of blood and horse sweat. A Medieval battlefield was a grim, grisly place, where knights were the heavy hitters.

Opposite: Armoured knights were the most powerful warriors of Medieval times.

Left: Flails were fearsome weapons based on a kind of farm tool.

NORMAN KNIGHTS

On 14 October 1066, the armies of King Harold of England and Duke William of Normandy faced off. Mounted knights were the backbone of the invading Norman army. Equipped with swords and long lances, these highly-trained horsemen were mobile killing machines.

DID YOU KNOW?
The Normans carried a shield shaped like a kite. This protected the upper body when riding on horseback.

1066

Bayeux Tapestry
The 70-metre (230-foot) long Bayeux Tapestry shows hundreds of Norman knights in action during their invasion of England and their great victory at the Battle of Hastings in 1066.

NORMAN ARMOUR

Arrows, swords, spears and flails could do a lot of damage. Troops needed to be well protected to survive a Medieval battle. Even the poorest foot soldier would have had a metal helm and shield. Richer warriors could afford a knee-length, short-sleeved shirt made of metal links, called chainmail. Sturdy gloves and boots protected any remaining bare skin.

FLAIL
The staff of a flail often held balls on chains.

DID YOU KNOW?
Chainmail comes from the French word *maille*, meaning 'net'.

MAIL HAUBERK
Armoured shirts were often split for horse riding.

KITE SHIELD
The kite shape protected the arm holding the horse's reins.

OPEN HELM
A nose bar protected the face from sword slashes.

1066 HASTINGS

It was early morning. The English soldiers hunkered behind their shields as the Norman cavalry thundered towards them. Rows of warriors pushed forward, forcing the defenders in the front line to stand their ground. Horses reared up, squealing in terror. Spears hit shields and fighters.

DID YOU KNOW?
The battle lasted all day – from 9 in the morning to when the sun set.

Left: William the Conqueror's half-brother, Bishop Odo, fought that day. He was armed with a club for bashing.

WINNING MOVE

- At Hastings, the Norman cavalry charged again and again, but the shield wall held.
- Only when the Normans faked a retreat, and King Harold's English forces chased, did the shield wall break.
- Finally, as the sun set, Harold was killed, and Duke William claimed the crown.

THE CRUSADES

Between 1096 and 1487, the Christian countries clashed with the Muslim world in a series of bloody battles known as the Crusades.

The Crusades were called by the Popes of Rome, who wanted Christian warriors to fight for control of an area in the Middle East called the Holy Land.

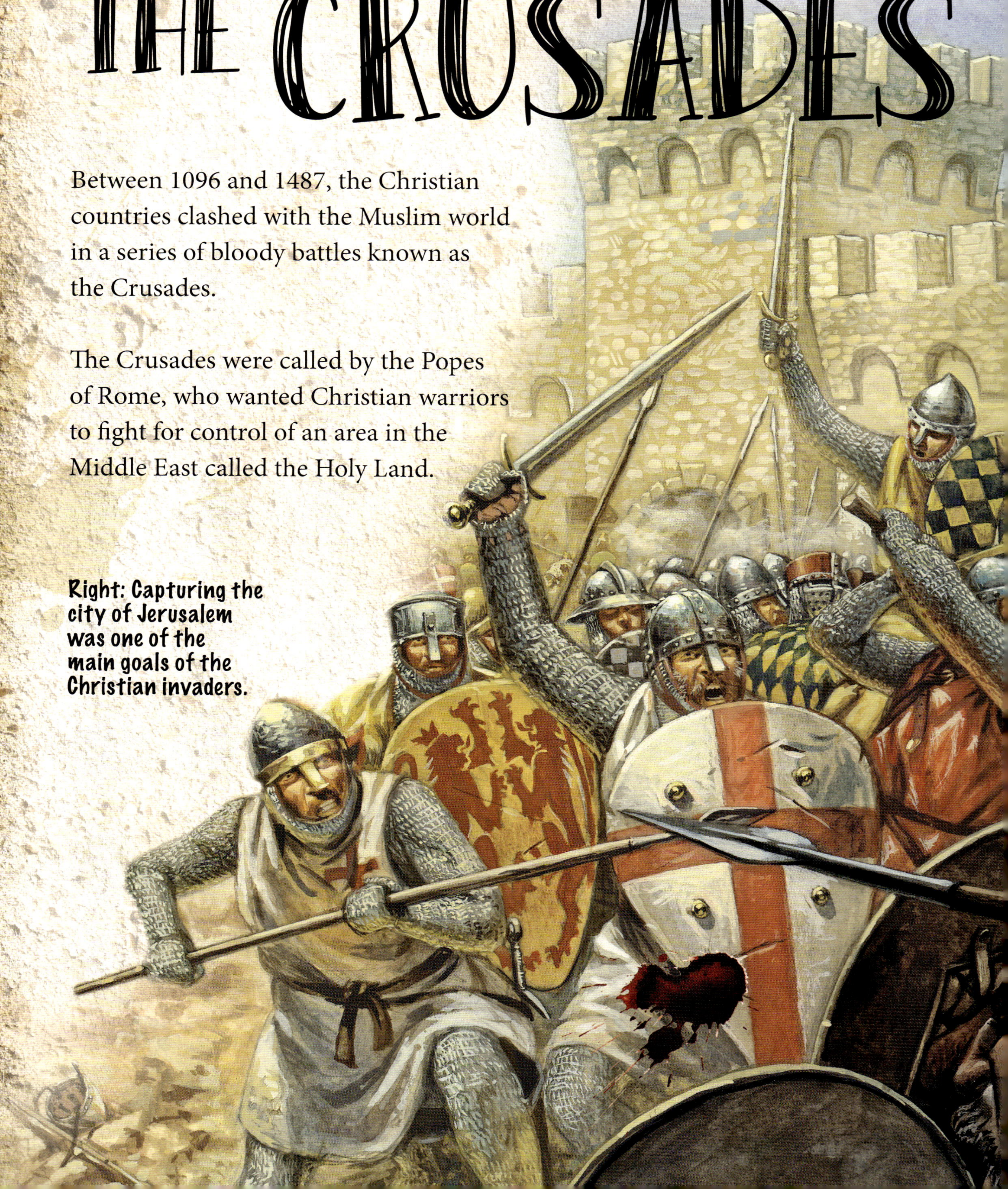

Right: Capturing the city of Jerusalem was one of the main goals of the Christian invaders.

1096–1487

CHRISTIAN KNIGHTS

- There were nine Crusades that tried to capture the Holy Land.
- Knights and soldiers from nearly every part of Europe went to fight in the Middle East.

DID YOU KNOW?

The Crusaders marked red crosses on their clothing and shields to show they were Christian.

KNIGHTS ON

CLOTHING

- Long shirts made of chainmail gave protection to the arms and body.
- A dress-like surcoat, marked with a red cross, identified the knight as a Crusader.

CRUSADE

In war two things are important: being well protected and being easy to recognise. The knight's shield did both of these jobs. Made of wood, leather or metal, shields gave protection from arrows and sword thrusts. A colourful pattern on the front helped the knight's comrades identify him in the heat of battle.

DID YOU KNOW?

Knights often dismounted for battle, fighting in tight groups for greater force and safety.

CHARGE!

CHARGING

Many things helped make a charge successful.

- The knights had to charge quickly to surprise the enemy.
- They had to stay close to one another so that they would hit the enemy hard together.
- Just before an attack, archers would shoot a hail of arrows that sent the enemy diving for cover.

Weather and the state of the battlefield had to be perfect for a cavalry charge to work. Charges did not happen very often, but when they did, they were terrifying. Charging soldiers used heavy lances to knock over foot soldiers. The horses trampled and scattered the enemy troops.

Charging knights needed skill and great bravery to keep the horses steady and in line. It was a race against death!

DID YOU KNOW?
A longbow arrow could easily punch through a knight's armour. The cavalry had to reach the enemy before the archers' arrows could hit them.

1212 BATTLE OF

Alfonso VIII was the king of Castile, in central Spain, but Muslim invaders had taken his land. In the spring of 1212, it was the king's turn for victory. Pope Innocent III had called a crusade, and Alfonso's neighbours, the kings of Navarre, Aragon and Portugal, had come to help.

Their troops crushed the army of the Muslim caliph Muhammad al-Nasir. The Spanish lost a few thousand knights that day. Caliph al-Nasir lost most of his army of 50,000 men.

DID YOU KNOW?

The Muslim forces were double the number of the Crusaders. Both the Crusaders and Muslims went into battle believing that their God would help them win.

LAS NAVAS

HOW THE BATTLE WAS WON

- The battlefield was wide and flat, suiting the charging Crusader cavalry.
- The Crusaders were heavily armoured, which helped them overcome the men of the caliph's army.

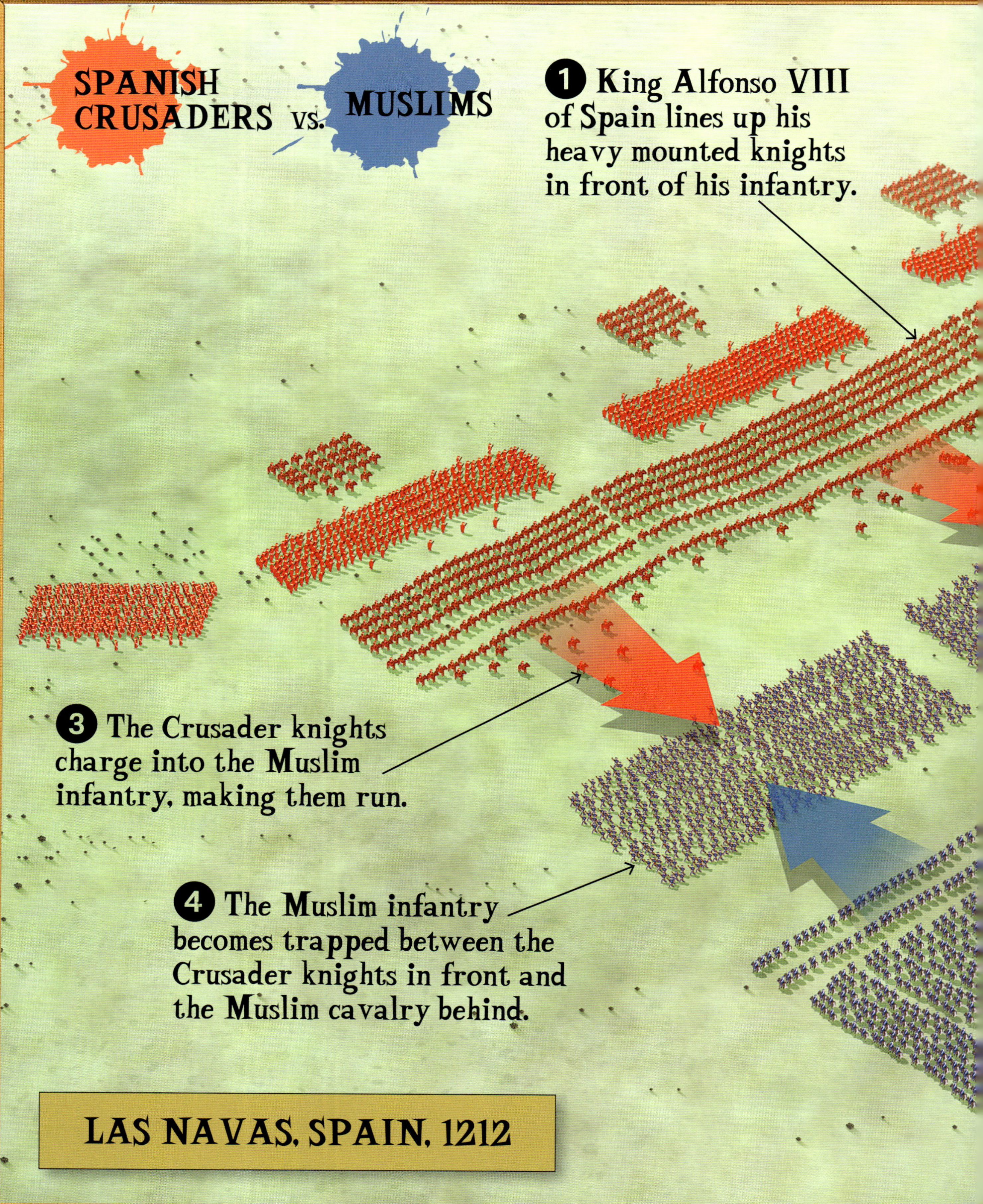
SPANISH CRUSADERS vs. MUSLIMS
1 King Alfonso VIII of Spain lines up his heavy mounted knights in front of his infantry.
3 The Crusader knights charge into the Muslim infantry, making them run.
4 The Muslim infantry becomes trapped between the Crusader knights in front and the Muslim cavalry behind.
LAS NAVAS, SPAIN, 1212

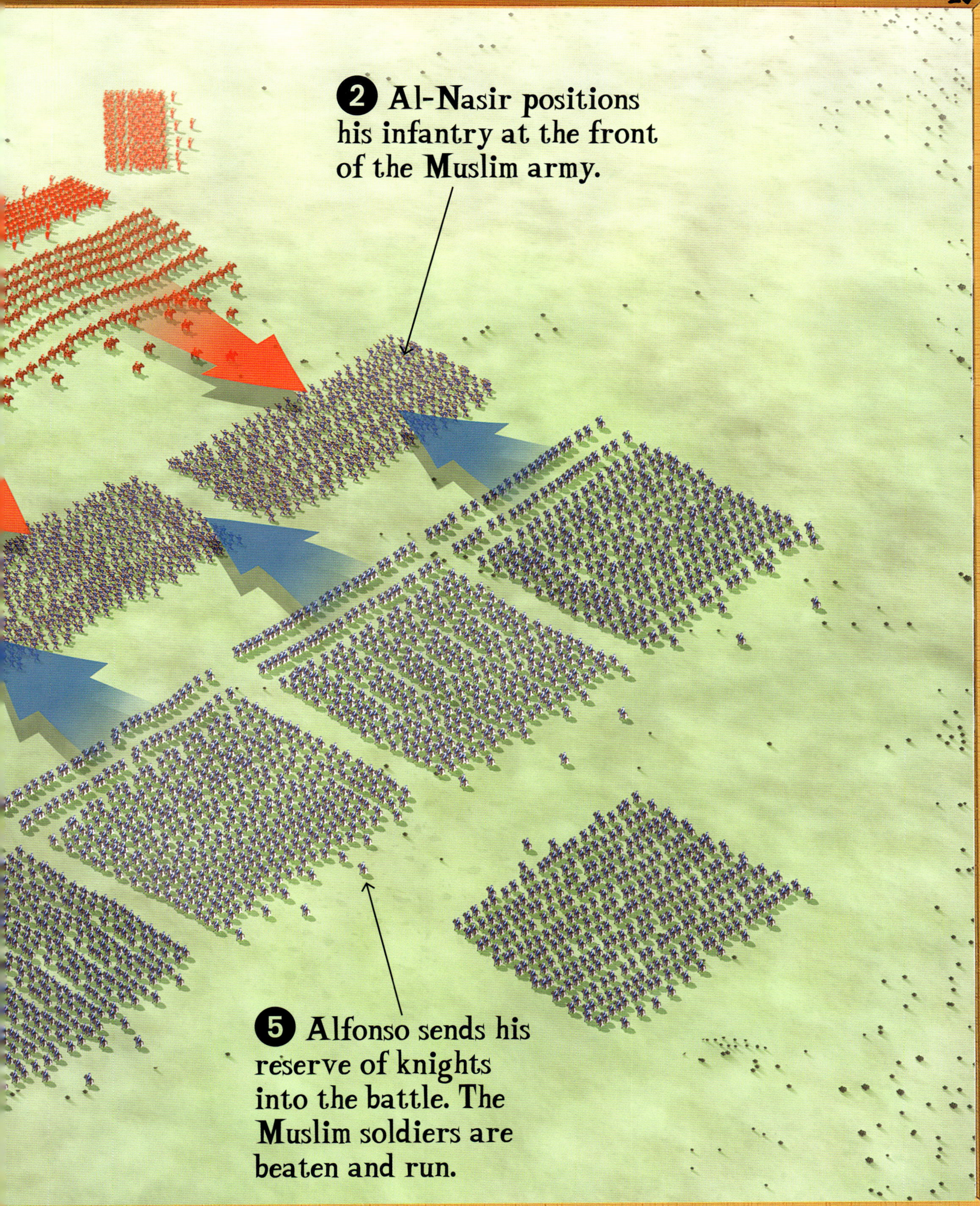
2 Al-Nasir positions his infantry at the front of the Muslim army.
5 Alfonso sends his reserve of knights into the battle. The Muslim soldiers are beaten and run.

TWO-HANDED AXE
This powerful weapon could slice a man in two.

PLATE ARMOUR

Films about knights do not get every detail right. Knights did not always wear shining armour. Full body armour was not developed until the 1400s – and it was very expensive. A suit of made-to-measure plate armour could cost as much as a Ferrari does today.

BOLTS AND STRAPS

- As the name suggests, plate armour was made up of plates of metal, linked by metal bolts and leather straps.
- It was very flexible and surprisingly light. The idea that knights had to be hoisted into their saddles with a wooden crane is totally untrue!

1300 – 1500

HELMET
The helmets included visors, which could be lifted up if the knight needed to show his whole face.

SHIELD
If a knight was beaten in battle, his spurs were removed and his shield was hung upside down.

DID YOU KNOW?
Full plate armour weighed between 16 and 25 kilograms (35 and 55 pounds) – about the same as the packs and weapons soldiers carry into battle today.

WEAPONS AND EQUIPMENT

Medieval knights used many different weapons, including long swords, flails, clubs, axes and lances for thrusting from horseback. Knights always sought to defeat their enemies in hand-to-hand combat. They did not rely on missile weapons, such as bows and arrows and slings. Missiles were used by foot soldiers.

KIT LIST (1400s):

- War horses x 3
- Full plate armour
- Longsword
- Stiletto (dagger)
- Lance/spear
- Shield
- Battle axe

1300 - 1500

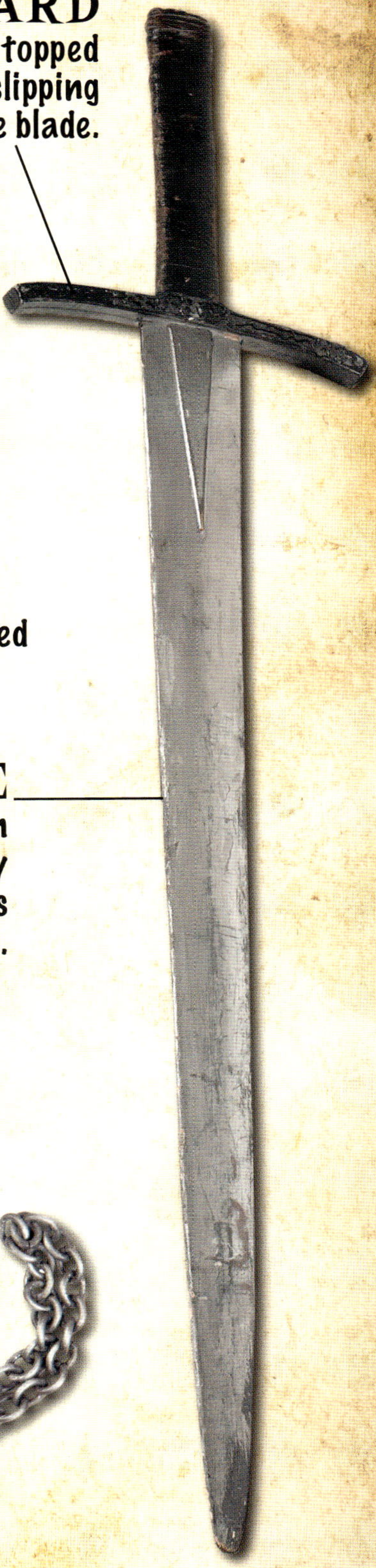

CROSS-GUARD
The T-shape stopped the hand from slipping down the blade.

GAUNTLET
Metal gloves protected the hands.

BLADE
The blade was sharp on both edges. It was usually about 76 centimetres (30 inches) long.

FLAIL
Spikes over 5 cm (2 inches) long were added to cause crushing damage.

SHIELD DEFENCE

- Knights would parry, or block, a blow from an enemy, using either shield or sword.
- Their shields could also be used to knock the opponent over.

KNIGHTS IN COMBAT

Knightly combat was a skill that depended on speed, fancy footwork and power. Combat manuals called *fechtbuchs* (fight books) taught squires (trainees) how to wrestle and how to fight with daggers, pole weapons and longswords, both on foot and on horseback.

DID YOU KNOW?

Boys began training to be knights at around eight years old. At the age of 21 they could be knighted. They would then have the right to carry a sword.

DID YOU KNOW?

Ball-and-chain flails had up to three balls. Often each ball was spiked.

FIGHTING WITH A FLAIL

Blunt instruments such as flails could be deadly! However, a flail needed space to be used well and hit an enemy with force.

Big Hit

The secret to success was short, controlled blows. In skilled hands, the flail became an extension of the knight's arm. After whipping out a flail to strike his enemy, a knight could knock the wind out of an opponent and even break bones.

TOOLS AS WEAPONS

Peasant armies fought with flails that were like farming tools. They had a long handle and a hinged striking end.

FIGHTING ON HORSEBACK

First came the charge, as the cavalry – armed with lances and spears – scattered troops before them. Then, knights would fight in close combat with swords and axes.

Horse Power

A knight's best weapon was his horse. A great horse weighed about half a tonne. So a knight needed to know how to handle his mount, move in the saddle and judge distances at top speeds.

DID YOU KNOW?

Knights spent years training at a hacking post to build up the muscle and stamina needed to swing a sword with great force.

MENACE WITH A MACE

As well as fighting with a sword, a knight could also hit with a mace, a kind of club. A mace blow could knock an opponent off his horse. A heavy blow could break bones, or give an enemy a headache and blurred vision, so that he could not carry on fighting.

COATS-OF-ARMS

- From the start of the 1300s, every knight's symbol was unique.
- The symbol that a knight wore on his armour was known as a coat-of-arms.
- Having a family coat-of-arms is still a matter of great pride to many people today.

HERALDRY

Knights fought for glory. So that they could be recognised in battle, their shields, helmets and surcoats were decorated with their family crest or personal symbol.

Above right: The coats-of-arms of English knights of the 14th century were made so they could be seen in battle.

DID YOU KNOW?

Heraldry is the study of ancient knightly badges, symbols and designs.

A TOURNEY

For rich lords and ladies, a tourney (tournament) was the best day of the year. Tourneys gave knights the chance to practise and show off their fighting skills, with mock battles and weapon fights. The melee, in which teams fought to be the 'last man standing', was very popular.

PLATE ARMOUR
Special tourney armour was made to reduce injuries.

LANCE
Up to three meters (ten feet) long.

GREAT HORSE
A horse could carry up to 181 kg (400 pounds) in weight.

LONGSWORD
The double-edged blade was 84 to 109 cm (33 to 43 inches).

1100 -1500

Left: Knights wrestle at a tournament in this 14th century artwork.

BRUTAL SPORT

- Early tourneys were so brutal that many knights were killed. Things became so bad that, in 1292, new rules made tourneys safer and more like sporting events.
- A successful tourney champion could expect honour, money and the cheers of the crowd!

JOUSTING

Jousting was designed to copy the battlefield cavalry charge. Armed with lances, and galloping at up to 80 kilometres per hour (50 miles per hour), knights tried to unhorse their opponents. Lances were lighter and blunter to make jousting safer. The joust became a test of skill, with knights competing to hit an opponent's shield, collect hoops or hit targets.

DID YOU KNOW?

Jousting continued long after knights vanished from the battlefield. In 1962 jousting became the official sport of Maryland in the United States.

CHAPTER 2

HORSE ARCHERS AND LIGHT CAVALRY

Bows and arrows were the machine guns of the Medieval world. An archer on horseback was a deadly weapon.

Right: When new, this Mongol cavalry helmet would have included a nose guard and a neck guard.

Opposite: Japanese yabusame archers of the 13th century were known for their skills as warriors.

DID YOU KNOW?
The knightly Chivalric Code of behaviour was based on ideas found in Arabian tales and poems.

ARAB LIGHT CAVALRY

If European knights were the Medieval world's battle tanks, then the Arab cavalry were its troop carriers. What the Arab cavalry lacked in armour, they made up for in speed.

Lightning Speed

Armed with a lance and sword, a light cavalryman covered the ground quickly, attacking the enemy wherever he saw weakness.

Left: Art from the 14th century sometimes showed Crusaders fighting the Saracen, or Muslim, cavalry.

1100 –1400

HORSE FLESH

- Arabian horses were bred from the best stock.
- They were famous for their speed and intelligence.

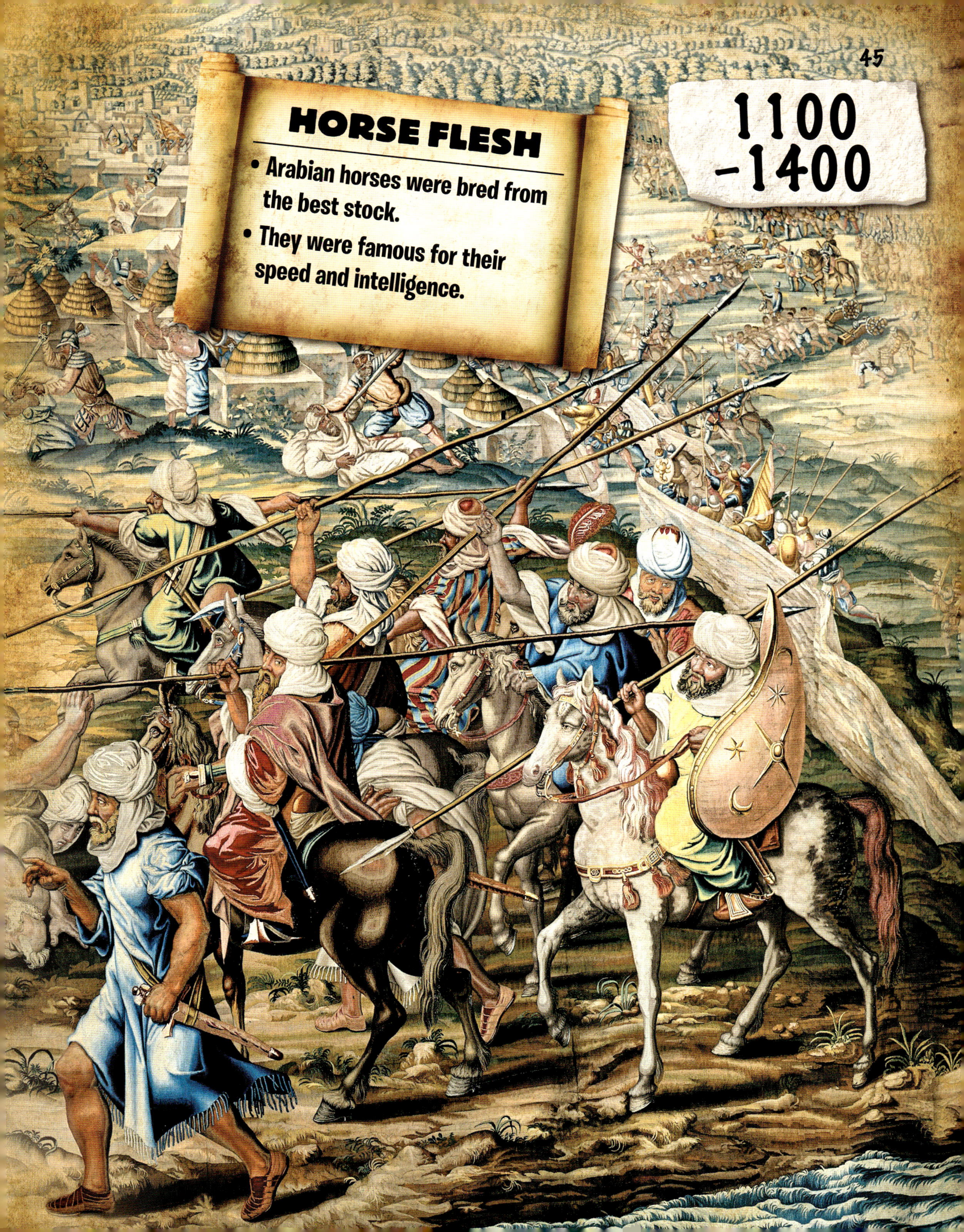

MONGOL CAVALRY

In the 13th century, the Mongols ruled the world's largest land empire. This was largely thanks to their incredible horsemanship. Sixty percent of a Mongol horde was made up of horse archers. The rest was light and heavy cavalry, often armed with lances or swords. It was an unbeatable combination.

"You cannot escape from the terror of our armies. Our horses are swift, our arrows sharp, our swords like thunderbolts."
(Ghengis Khan's grandson Hulagu Khan, 1260)

1200 - 1300

Left: When his father, the khan (chief), was murdered, Temüjin of the Borjigin was thrown out of his tribe. This poor, homeless boy later became Ghengis, Great Khan of the Mongol Empire.

DID YOU KNOW?

Horde **comes from the Mongolian word,** ***ordu,*** **which means 'field army'.**

MONGOL CAVALRY EQUIPMENT

In battle, the Mongols relied on speed, which meant travelling light.

ARMOUR

- Mongols wore lamellar armour. This was made from small squares of iron or hardened leather.
- Underneath the armour, the men wore silk shirts. If they were shot, the silk would wrap around the arrowhead, making it easier to pull out.

COMPOSITE BOW
A mixed bow was made of horn, wood and animal tissue (sinew).

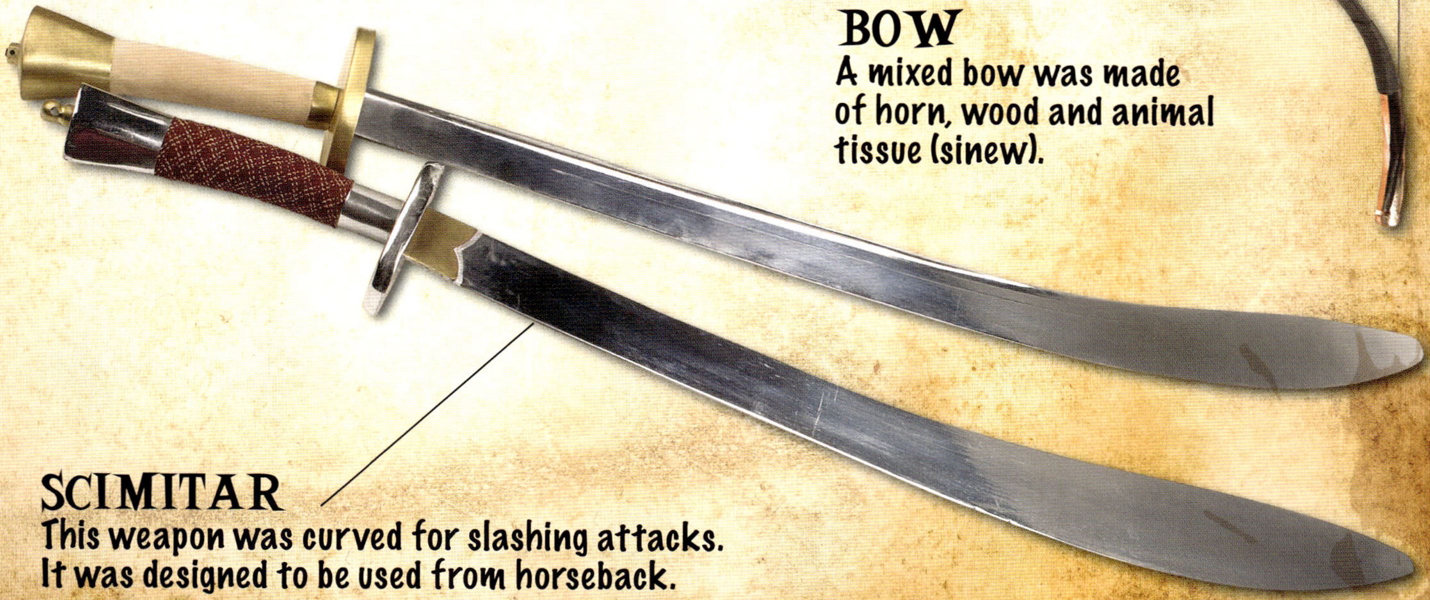

SCIMITAR
This weapon was curved for slashing attacks. It was designed to be used from horseback.

DID YOU KNOW?

After capturing cities, Mongols would take any engineers prisoner. These men became part of their army and were used to make their siege weapons.

HELMET
Headgear was made of leather or metal, depending on how rich a soldier was.

LAMELLAR ARMOUR
Fighters in the heavy cavalry wore their armour over a long coat.

HORSES

A Mongol warrior's horses were his life. Every cavalryman had at least four horses. They gave the warrior everything he needed, from horse hair, used for ropes, to dung, which was burnt instead of wood.

Small and Tough

When food was hard to find, warriors could drink mare's milk mixed with horse blood. However, these tough little horses were at their most useful on the battlefield. They could move quickly, dashing between groups of foot soldiers, while their riders fired hails of arrows.

DID YOU KNOW?

Mongol horsemen changed horses regularly. This meant they could ride up to 160 kilometres (100 miles) in a day.

Above: Beautiful, fast Mongol horses would sweep across the Mongolian plains.

BALANCING ACT

Horse archers controlled their horses using their knees. This kept the archers' hands free to fire their bows.

HORSE ARCHERS

European archers could fire ten longbow arrows a minute, but they had to stand in one spot to shoot well. On horseback, Mongol archers could cover more of the battlefield and kill more of the enemy. Their bows were small and light. So, skill rather than raw power was the secret to their success.

Below: Mongol archers were so feared that archery was banned after China conquered Mongolia.

DID YOU KNOW?

European bows are pulled using the forefinger and middle finger. Mongol bows are pulled with the thumb.

When retreating, Mongol horse archers would often turn in the saddle to fire at the enemy behind. The ancient Parthians made this tactic, called the 'Parthian shot', famous.

HORSE ARCHER FACTS

- Archers carried two bows. A heavier bow with a longer range was used on foot.
- A horse archer could fire an arrow over 300 metres (1,000 feet) and hit a target at up to 174 m (570 feet).
- Archers carried different types of arrows: some for piercing armour, some for shooting fire.

1241

LEGNICA

The Mongol leader, Batu Khan, made his demands: surrender your land and a tenth of your wealth, or die!

Crushing Victory

On 9 April 1241, Batu's 20,000-strong horde crushed Duke Henry II's Silesian army. The victory was so unexpected that people believed the Mongols were not just men, but supernatural beings.

Right: Mongol cavalry (left) attacked Christian knights (right) at Legnica. On Henry's side were Polish, German and French knights.

A GRISLY COUNT

The Mongols used fear as a weapon.

- After Legnica, the Mongols killed everyone in the area.
- To count the dead, they cut the ears off corpses, filling nine large sacks.

DID YOU KNOW?

Before the battle, a stone fell from a church and almost killed Duke Henry as he marched out of the city of Legnica.

CHRISTIAN KNIGHTS vs. MONGOLS

1 The Silesian knights charge into the Mongol light cavalry.

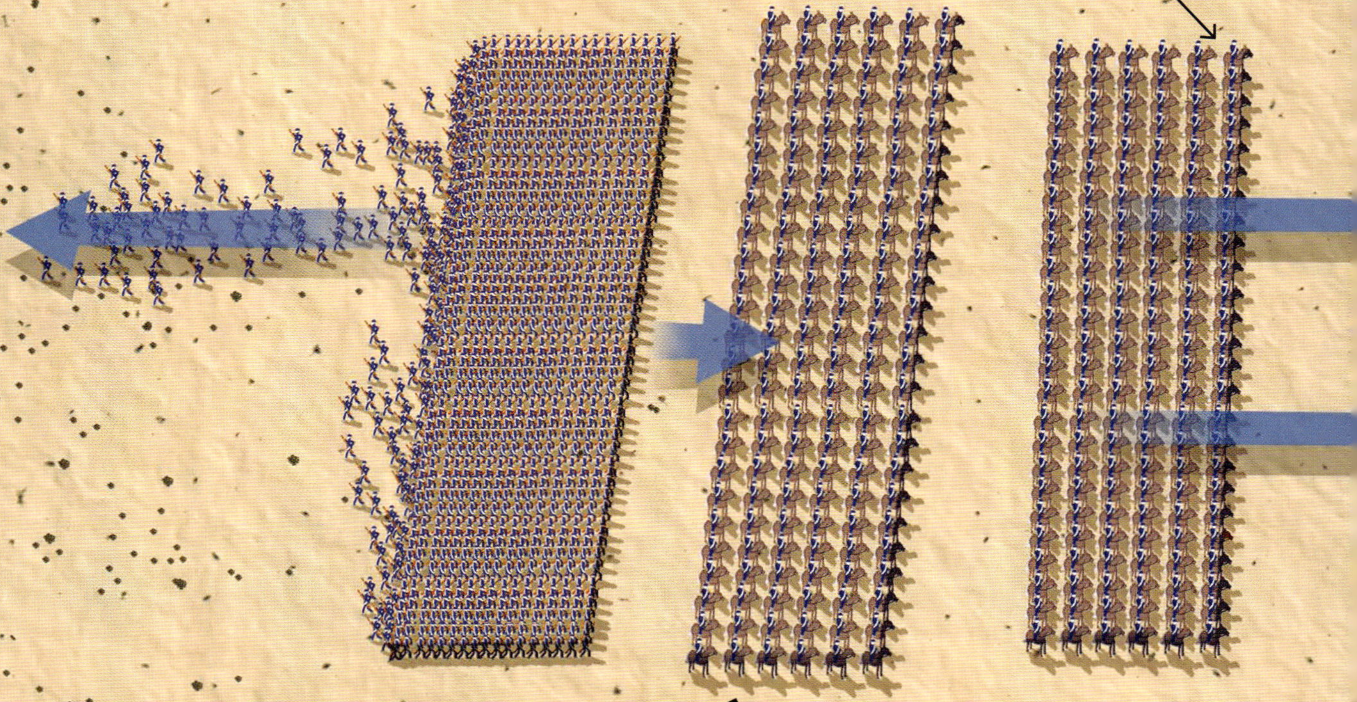

2 They are followed by a second wave of knights.

LEGNICA, POLAND, 1241

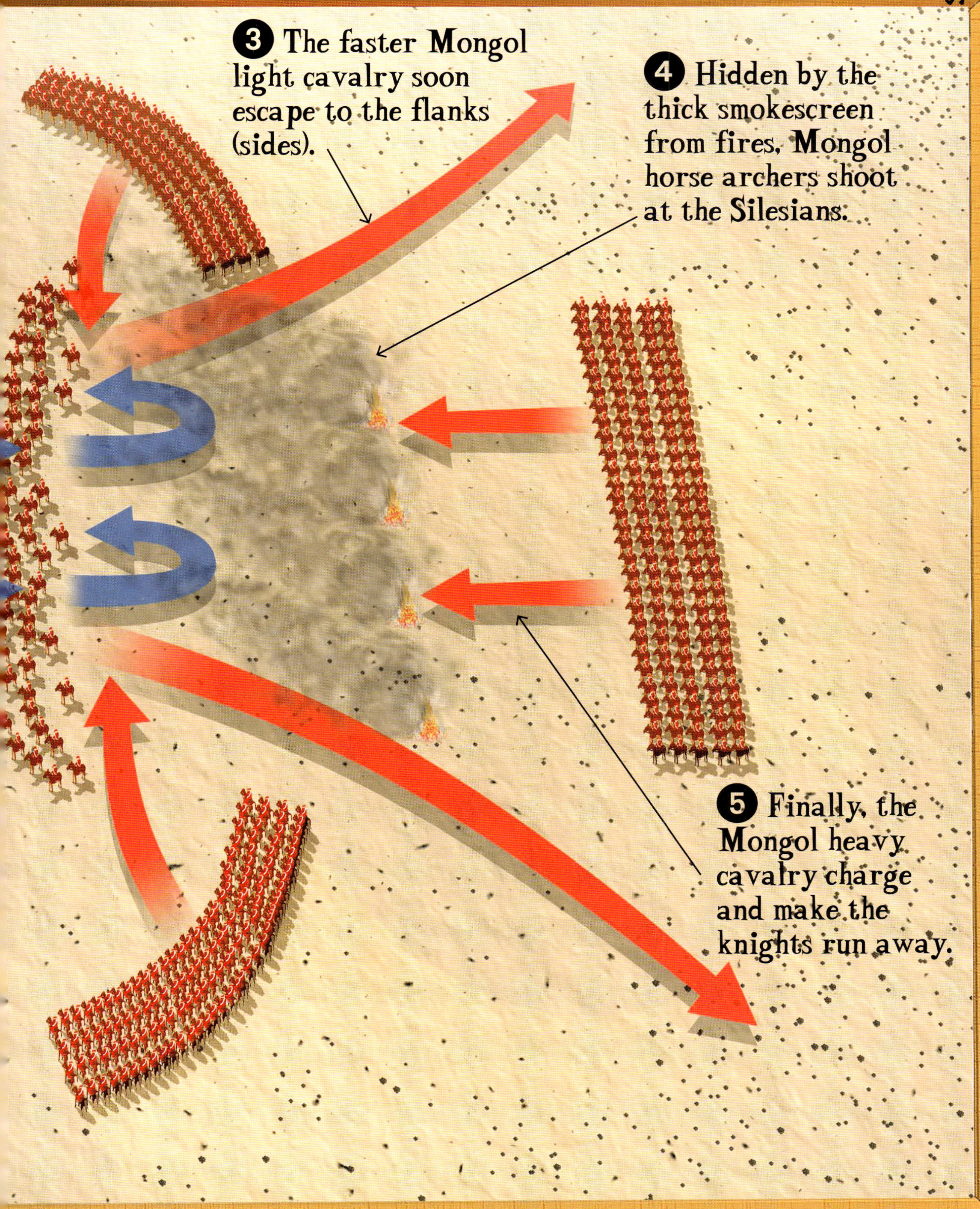

3 The faster Mongol light cavalry soon escape to the flanks (sides).
4 Hidden by the thick smokescreen from fires, Mongol horse archers shoot at the Silesians.
5 Finally, the Mongol heavy cavalry charge and make the knights run away.

1100 - 1500

SAMURAI WARRIOR

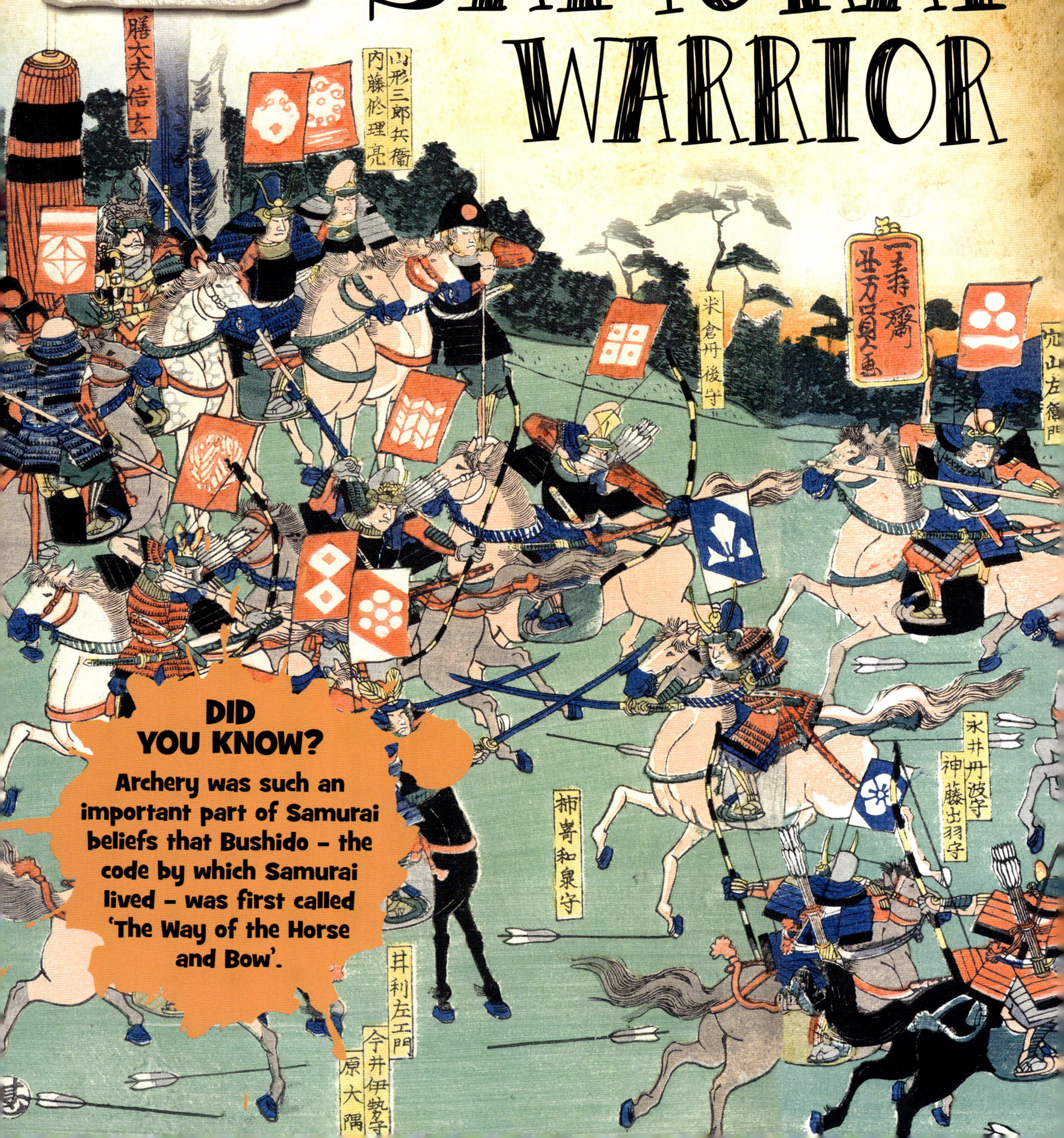

DID YOU KNOW?

Archery was such an important part of Samurai beliefs that Bushido – the code by which Samurai lived – was first called 'The Way of the Horse and Bow'.

Samurai believed in honour on the battlefield. A 'civilized' battle would open with boasts from the clan leaders. After an exchange of arrows, the greatest Samurai would charge into combat, while lesser warriors waited their turn. However, in reality the fighting would start any number of ways.

Above: Samurai armour changed over time, but the bows remained the same.

UNCIVIL WAR

During the Battle of Kurikara (1183), the Taira and Minamoto clans agreed to settle their differences in a civilized way. Halfway through the battle, the Minamoto clan changed the rules, using stampeding cattle to drive their enemy off a cliff.

Left: In the 1400s, Samurai on horseback fought with bows, pole weapons, and swords in a pitch battle.

KATANA
This light, curved sword was made to be incredibly sharp.

SAMURAI WEAPONS

Although early Samurai used the bow, by the 13th century, the curved *katana* sword had become their main weapon. These were often worn with a smaller *wakizashi* sword. Together, the pair were called *daishō* (meaning 'big little').

'Big Little'

They were more than just weapons. Bushido taught that the Samurai's soul was in his sword.

YUMI
This bow might be up to 203 cm (80 inches) in length – which was often longer than the archer using it.

KIT LIST (1400)

- Katana (curved sword)
- Tanto (small dagger)
- Naginata (pole weapon)
- Yumi (bow)
- Armour

NAGINATA
The blade of this pole weapon was often 38 cm (15 inches) long.
KATANA
A Samurai kept a 70-cm (27-inch) long sword at his side.

ONE-TO-ONE COMBAT

Medieval writers loved to tell tales of heroes locked in single combat. History has not always remembered the names of the individual soldiers, but it is clear that each one fought for survival.

DID YOU KNOW?
The bodyguards of the Anglo-Saxon kings were called *huscarls*. They were armed with a sword or an axe.

CHAPTER 3

FOOT SOLDIERS

Swords swing, pikes stab out. Someone sidesteps a flail, and stumbles into the tip of a halberd. On a Medieval battlefield, foot soldiers faced – and dished out – death, up close.

Opposite: Pikemen fought with their pikes in close quarters.

Left: Shields of the 10th century were made for both defending and attacking.

FIGHTING SMART

In Viking sagas, warriors did not fight fair; they fought smart.

- Spears were used to pole-vault over rivers.
- Shields were ridden like sleds.
- Untying an opponent's belt so their trousers fell down was also a popular tactic!

Below: In the 15th century, men-at-arms would fight to the death. During combat, they would look for a gap in the enemy's armour.

Skill and Luck

Men-at-arms would be trained to fight in single combat. They would practice blows, defences and movements over and over.

Left: Huscarls fight with a sword and axe in hand-to-hand combat.

EQUIPMENT

The kit of the infantrymen did not change for almost 1,000 years. A Roman centurion, living around 100 BCE, would have recognised most of the equipment used by a huscarl at Hastings.

Home Comforts

Not every piece of equipment was designed to kill. Some items, such as cutlery and money pouches, just made life easier.

SHIELD

HELMET

BUCKLER
Used in combat to turn aside sword blows.

DID YOU KNOW?
Medieval people did not have forks. They used spoons, and they had knives to cut and stab their meat.

A SOLDIER'S KIT BAG

Wars could last for years, so soldiers had to be able to look after themselves and their equipment. Common kit bags included:

- steel, flint and tinder for starting a fire
- needles and thread to repair clothes
- water pouches, cups and bowls

DAGGER and SCABBARD

PURSE
For carrying money.

BELT and POUCH

KNIFE and SCABBARD
For hunting and cooking.

RICH MAN, POOR MAN

- Sword: rich man's weapon, as it was costly and its use required skill
- Axe: easy for both rich and poor to use
- Spear: poor soldier's weapon; good for stabbing armoured men
- Halberd: poor man's weapon; had a spear's reach with the crushing power of an axe

HAND WEAPONS

Hand weapons were made to cause the most horrifying damage – beheadings, smashed skulls, broken bones, lost limbs – in the shortest time.

HARD HITTERS

Many soldiers could fight on with an arrow wound. Most deaths were caused by blows to the head from heavy, blunt weapons.

DID YOU KNOW?

At 16 years old, King Henry V of England was hit in the face by an arrow – but he survived.

FIGHTING WITH AN AXE

BESERKERS

"The Norsemen rushed forward without armour, as mad as wolves, as strong as bears, biting their shields ... they killed with one blow .... This was called berserkering."
(Snorri Sturluson, 1225.)

In an age when most items were made of wood, every home had an axe. Designed to cut and split trees, these simple tools became terrifying weapons on a battlefield. Longer axes allowed soldiers to attack from a distance. Shorter axes were faster and easier to aim. Both were brutal.

DID YOU KNOW?

Viking axes were 1 m (40 inches) long and could behead a horse with one stroke.

SHIELD WALL

A shield wall relied on nerves of steel – and trust. The warriors in the wall knew their lives depended on those standing beside them to hold their ground together.

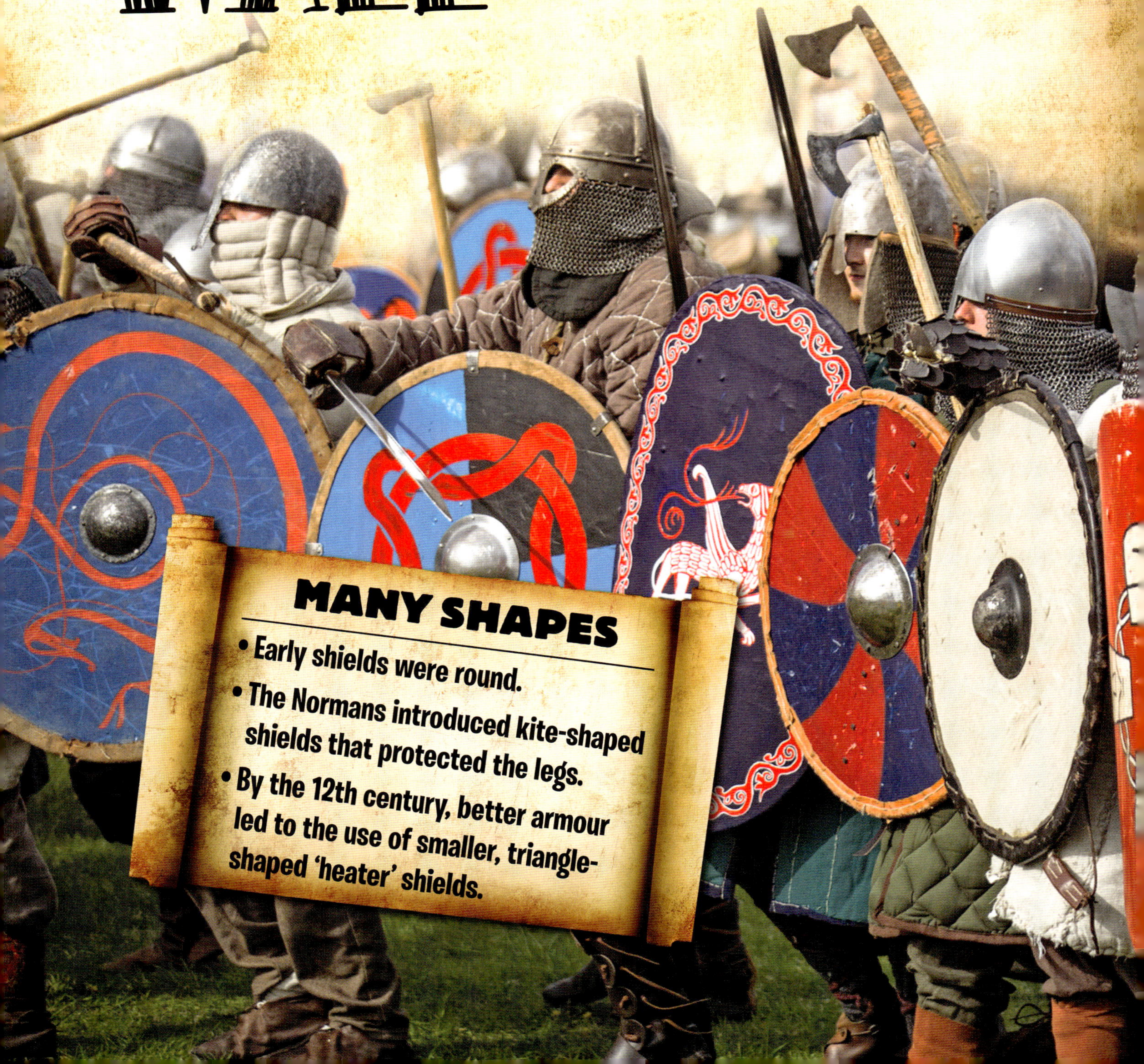

MANY SHAPES

- Early shields were round.
- The Normans introduced kite-shaped shields that protected the legs.
- By the 12th century, better armour led to the use of smaller, triangle-shaped 'heater' shields.

Hold Your Ground!

Short swords and spears stabbed the enemy through gaps in the shield wall. Each warrior stabbed left or right, protecting the man next to him.

DID YOU KNOW?

Shield walls were used by Egyptian, Roman, Greek and Celtic armies in ancient times.

Below: A shield wall was a fearsome form of defence.

PITCH BATTLE

The challenge was to choose ground and hold it. The aim of every Medieval king, general or clan leader was to break the enemy's troops and drive them from the battlefield.

A Waiting Game

After the two sides had agreed when and where their armies would meet, a pitch battle could take days to start. No one wanted to be the first to move, as it was much easier to defend than attack.

DID YOU KNOW?

Many people were killed as they lay wounded on the ground after the battle had finished.

Right: Knights and men-at-arms struggle in a hand-to-hand melee.

DEATH OR GLORY

- European commanders wanted to be seen on the battlefield leading their men. However, troops could panic if their leader was killed.
- Mongol leaders directed battles from a distance. They did not care about personal glory, just victory.

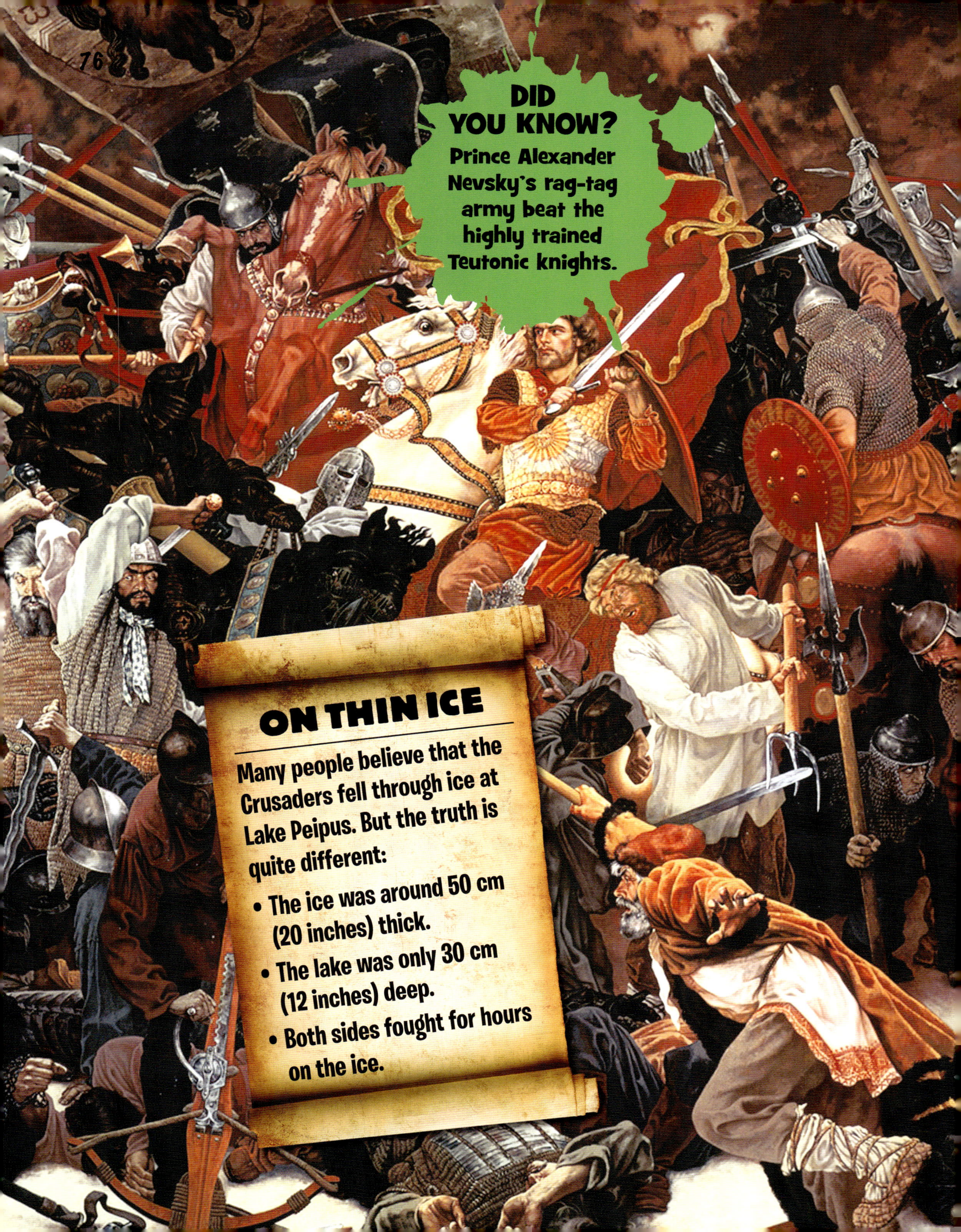

DID YOU KNOW?

Prince Alexander Nevsky's rag-tag army beat the highly trained Teutonic knights.

ON THIN ICE

Many people believe that the Crusaders fell through ice at Lake Peipus. But the truth is quite different:

- The ice was around 50 cm (20 inches) thick.
- The lake was only 30 cm (12 inches) deep.
- Both sides fought for hours on the ice.

TEUTONIC KNIGHTS vs. RUSSIANS

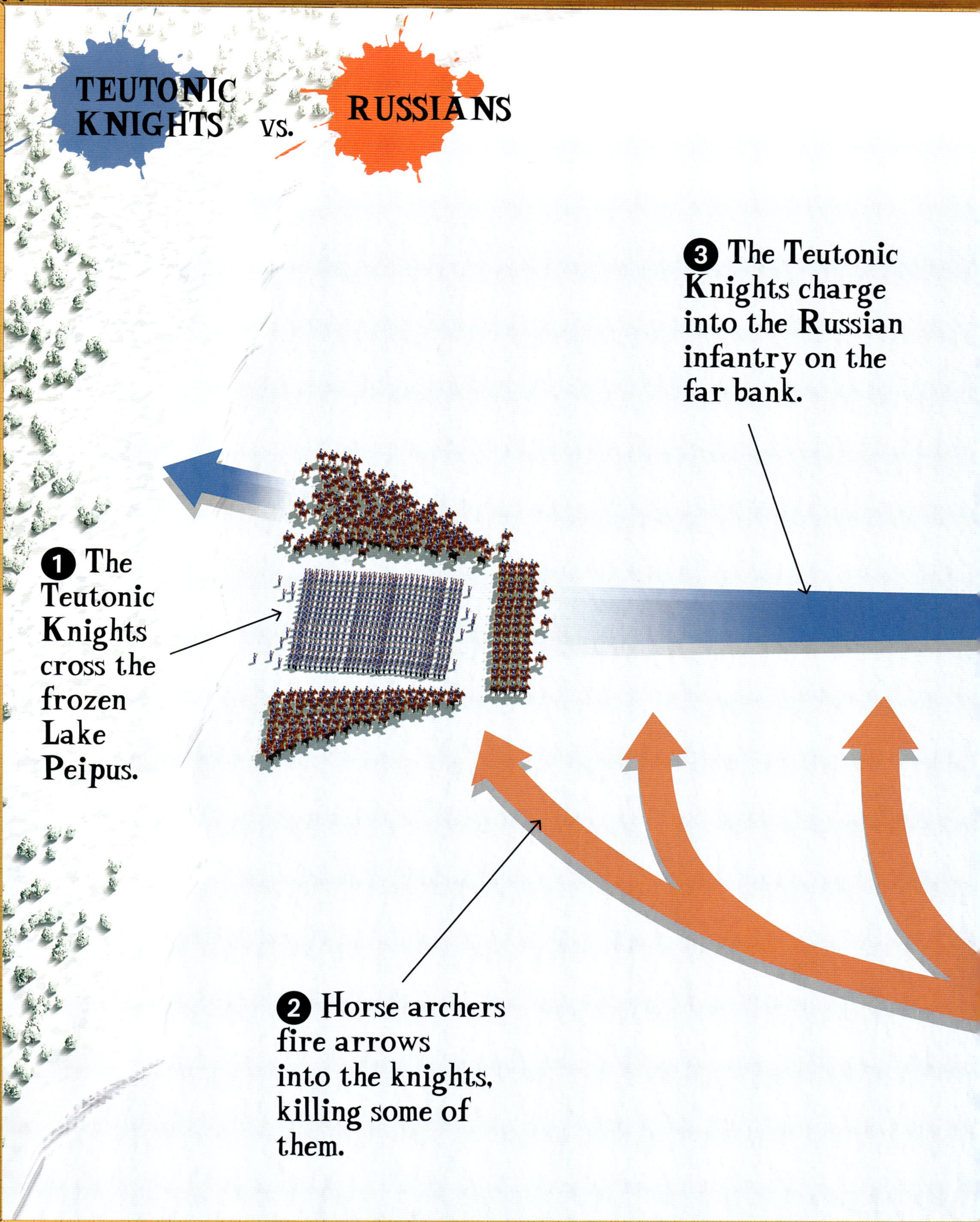

1242

LAKE PEIPUS

The wind was bitingly cold. Ranks of spearmen and bowmen stood, silently, on the shores of the frozen Lake Peipus. To the left and right, heavy cavalry and horse archers waited, their hot breath forming wispy clouds. As the enemy Crusaders hit the ice, their horses slowed and Nevsky's Russian army closed for the kill.

Left: At Lake Peipus, the Teutonic knights underestimated the Russian infantry, whose fierce hand-to-hand fighting tired the knights.

4 Alexander Nevsky sends his cavalry to attack the Teutonic Knights on both flanks (sides).

5 Fighting for two hours on the frozen lake, the exhausted knights are now trapped, and many die or are taken prisoner.

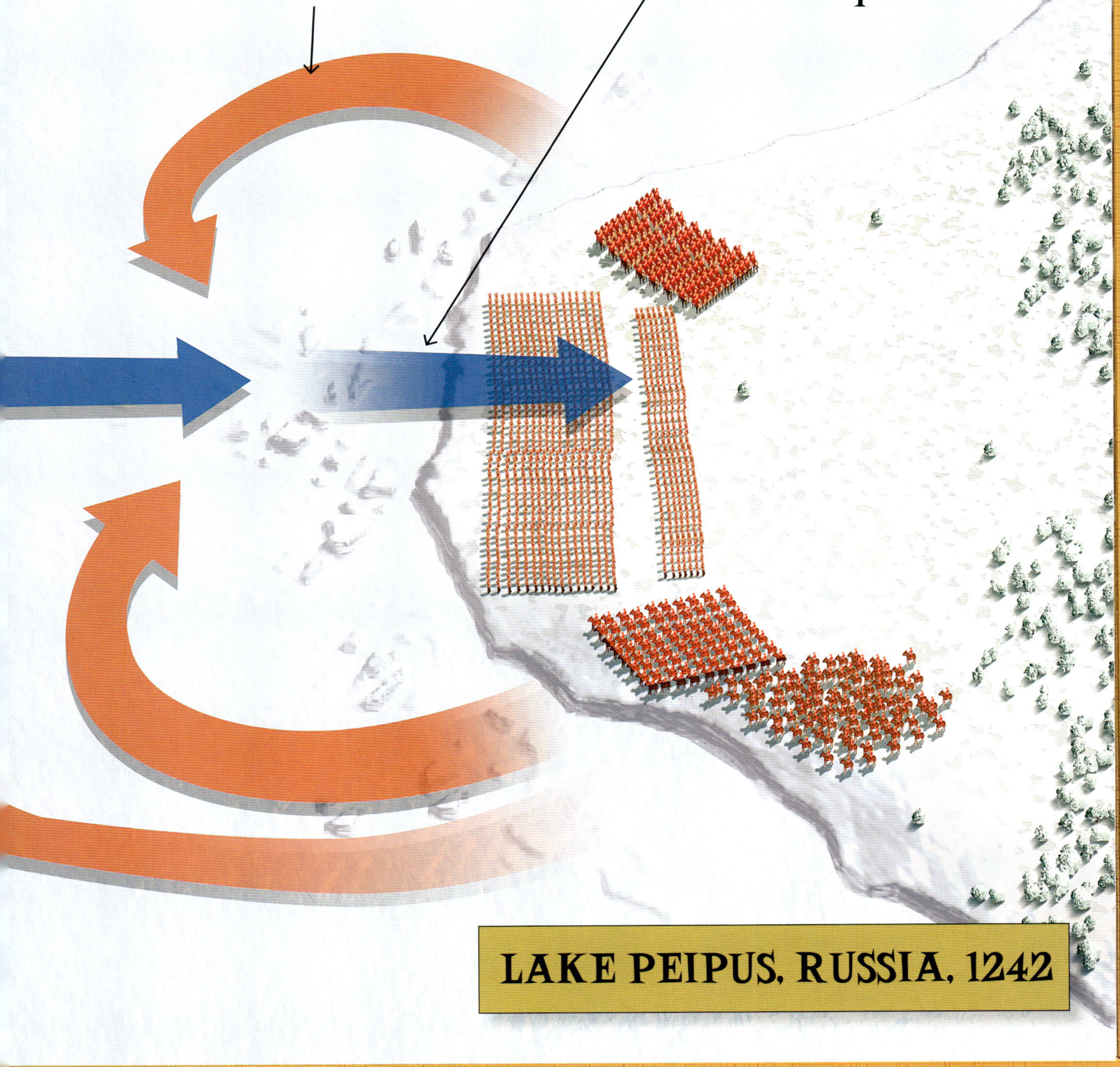

1300s FIGHTING SHIP TO SHIP

Cannons would roar and wood splinter as ships closed on each other, like mounted knights at a tourney.

Floating Fortresses

Our ideas about sea battles are based on the battles fought in the 1700s. However, Medieval sea battles were much less dramatic. Defending ships were used like floating castles, and chained together in lines.

FLOATING BATTLEFIELD

- Ships lined up near the coast.
- As ships drew close, archers fired from wooden towers on the decks.
- Foot soldiers then tried to board and capture the enemy's ship.

Below: At the battle of Sluys in 1340, more than 300 English and French ships fought each other.

DID YOU KNOW?

Cogs were warships with flat bottoms and high sides.

WOMEN WARRIORS

Right: Joan of Arc's presence inspired the French troops, even though she never fought in battle.

MAID OF ORLÉANS

Joan of Arc (1412–1431) made it her mission to drive the English invaders from France. Her inspiration, she said, came from God. However, her bravery was short-lived. Aged 19, she was burned at the stake for cross-dressing, which was a crime then.

DID YOU KNOW?
Viking warrior Freydís Eiríksdóttir terrified the enemy by beating her bare chest with her sword.

From Viking shield maidens to warrior queens like Thyra of Denmark, women fighters were scary.

Secret Soldiers

Upper class ladies were protected by their social class and could fight openly. Ordinary women disguised themselves as men to become soldiers.

PIKEMEN AND HALBERDIERS

HALBERD

The axe sat on a 2 m (6 foot) long shaft. The back of the axe had a 'thorn' used to pull knights off horses.

PIKE

The spear was often 3 to 6 m (10 to 20 feet) long and was thrust at an enemy.

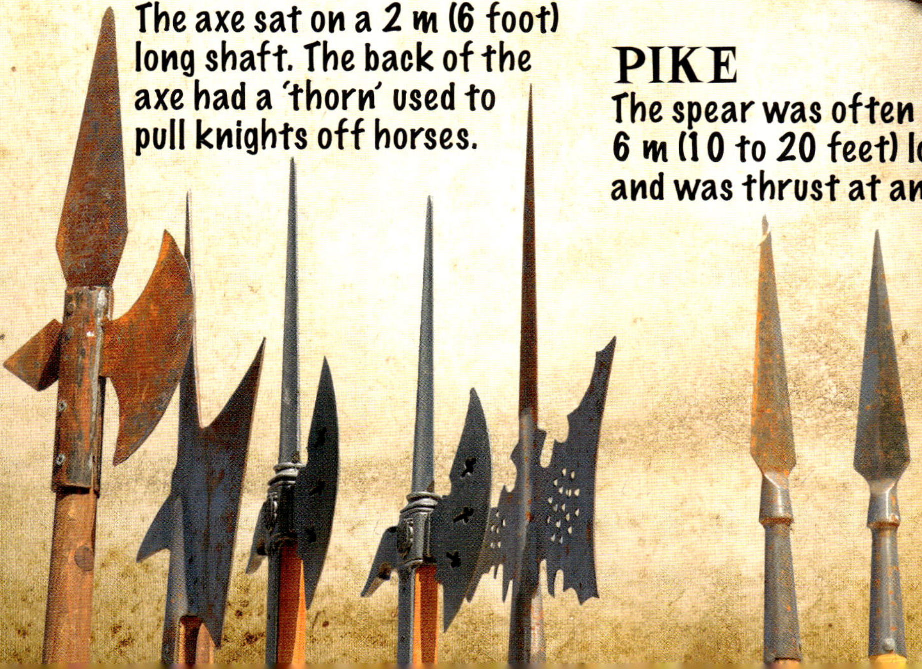

1400s

For lightly armoured foot soldiers, it made sense to keep as much distance as possible from the enemy. Polearms, such as pikes and halberds, were a great defence from swinging swords and charging horses.

Looking for Trouble
In very close combat, polearms were difficult to use. So pikemen also carried daggers or flails. A pikeman without a pike was usually in trouble!

DID YOU KNOW?
As two-handed weapons became popular, the shield wall was replaced by the pike square, which was often set up as ten rows of ten men.

CHAPTER 4

ARCHERS

In modern warfare, machine gunners are used to pin down enemy troops. Archers did the same job on a Medieval battlefield, but with greater accuracy.

Opposite: A Middle Eastern archer pulls back the string and aims his bow.

Right: During the Hundred Years' War (1337–1453), the skills of the English archers helped to win battles.

FIRING A

BOW

Place the arrow, draw the string… release. The energy from the draw pushes the arrow forward, creating one of the world's simplest and deadliest machines.

DID YOU KNOW?
An English law from 1514 said that all men aged 7 to 40 must practice archery and own a bow.

Practice Makes Perfect

It takes years to learn how to fire a bow well. The best method of firing depends on the type of bow being used.

Opposite: In Eastern Europe, both European and Mongol-style bows (shown here) were used.

SHOOTING A BOW

- Decide if your sight is better in your left or right eye.
- If 'right-eyed', use a right-handed bow. Hold with your left hand; draw with your right.
- Place the arrow, and raise the bow.
- Pull the string back to arm's length.
- Relax your hold to fire.

TYPES OF BOW

Bows have different shapes and sizes and can be made of different materials. How a bow is made is as important as the skill of the archer using it.

The Same, But Different

Self bows are made from one piece of material. Composite bows are made by putting together different materials. Most composite bows are recurve. This means they have curved tips. Reflex bows are shaped like a letter C.

CROSSBOW

Crossbows (left) fired powerful bolts in place of arrows. They were invented in China in the 4th century BCE.

SELF BOW

Like this self bow (right), all bows have a stave (body) and a string.

DID YOU KNOW?

If your surname is Bowyer, your family may have been bow makers.

CHOOSING A BOW

There are many bow designs, and each has its advantages.

- Power: longbow
- Lightness: composite bow
- Speed: recurve bow
- Easy to use: crossbow
- Easy to carry: Reflex bow

LONGBOW

Longbows (left) were made from one piece of wood, up to 1.8 m (6 feet) long.

THE CROSSBOW

By the 1400s, archers had become the heroes of the Medieval battlefield. They were respected and well paid. It took years to learn an archer's skills. However, crossbows could be fired with less fuss. They were point-and-fire weapons.

TYPES

- Claw crossbow: A claw or hook was used to grip the string.
- Stirrup crossbow: Bowman loaded the bow by placing a foot in the stirrup.
- Windlass crossbow: Its string was wound tight with a hook.

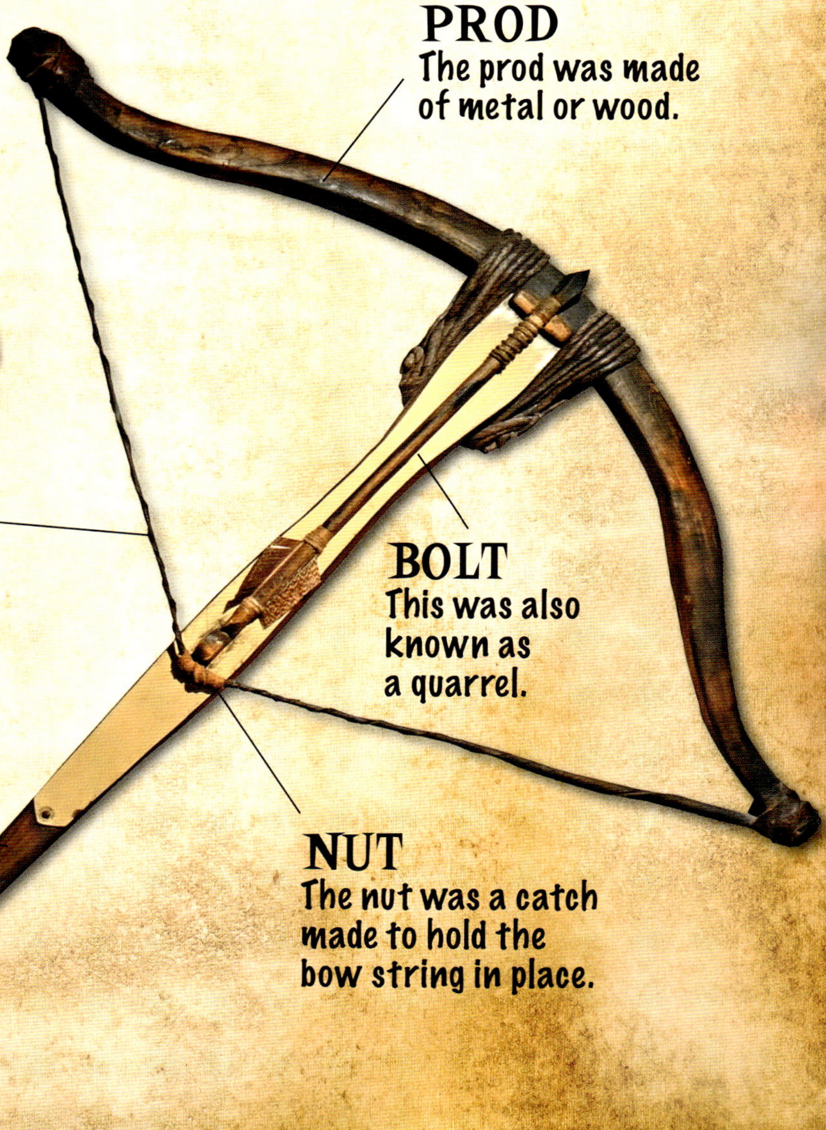

Pure Power

The more energy needed to pull a bow, the further an arrow will fly and the harder it will hit. Crossbows were hard to pull, making them powerful weapons.

DID YOU KNOW?
Crossbows had a maximum range of 320 to 350 m (350 to 380 yards).

Right: A device like a horse's stirrup on the prod made the bow easier to pull.

THE LONGBOW

Once, knights fought knights and infantry fought infantry. During the Hundred Years' War, all that changed. The arrows of the English longbowmen cut down many French nobles.

Power and Glory

The skills of longbowmen scared the aristocracy so much that laws were passed to make sure that the men armed with longbows did not become too powerful.

ARROWHEAD FACTS

BARBED: hard to remove

BODKIN: amour-piercing

BROAD-HEAD: wide and flat for cutting flesh

Below: Longbowmen could fire a volley of arrows. A longbow could easily fire a range of 230 m (250 yards).

TWO-FINGERED SIGN

According to Jean de Wavrin (1398–1474), the French threatened to cut off enemy archers' fingers. Legend says that the 'two-fingered salute' shown opposite was based on English archers showing the French they still had their fingers.

DID YOU KNOW?

Drawing a longbow was like pulling a weight of around 64 kg (140 pounds).

ARROWS AT AGINCOURT

The battle opened. A cloud of arrows was fired. Horses and men toppled into the thick mud. Men raised their shields and stumbled forward.

Below: Longbowmen could fire six arrows per minute. This created a hail of arrows that looked like sharp rain.

Men and Mud

At the battle of Agincourt in 1415, the French men-at-arms were slowed down by their own numbers and the thick mud. This made them easy targets for the English archers.

1415

DID YOU KNOW?
At Agincourt, English archers ran out of arrows and had to pluck them from dead bodies.

WHO WAS THERE?

Fighting for Henry V, King of England:
- 4,950 archers
- 750 men-at-arms on foot

For Charles d'Albret, Constable of France:
- 7,000 men-at-arms on horseback
- 15,000 soldiers on foot
- 3,000 crossbowmen

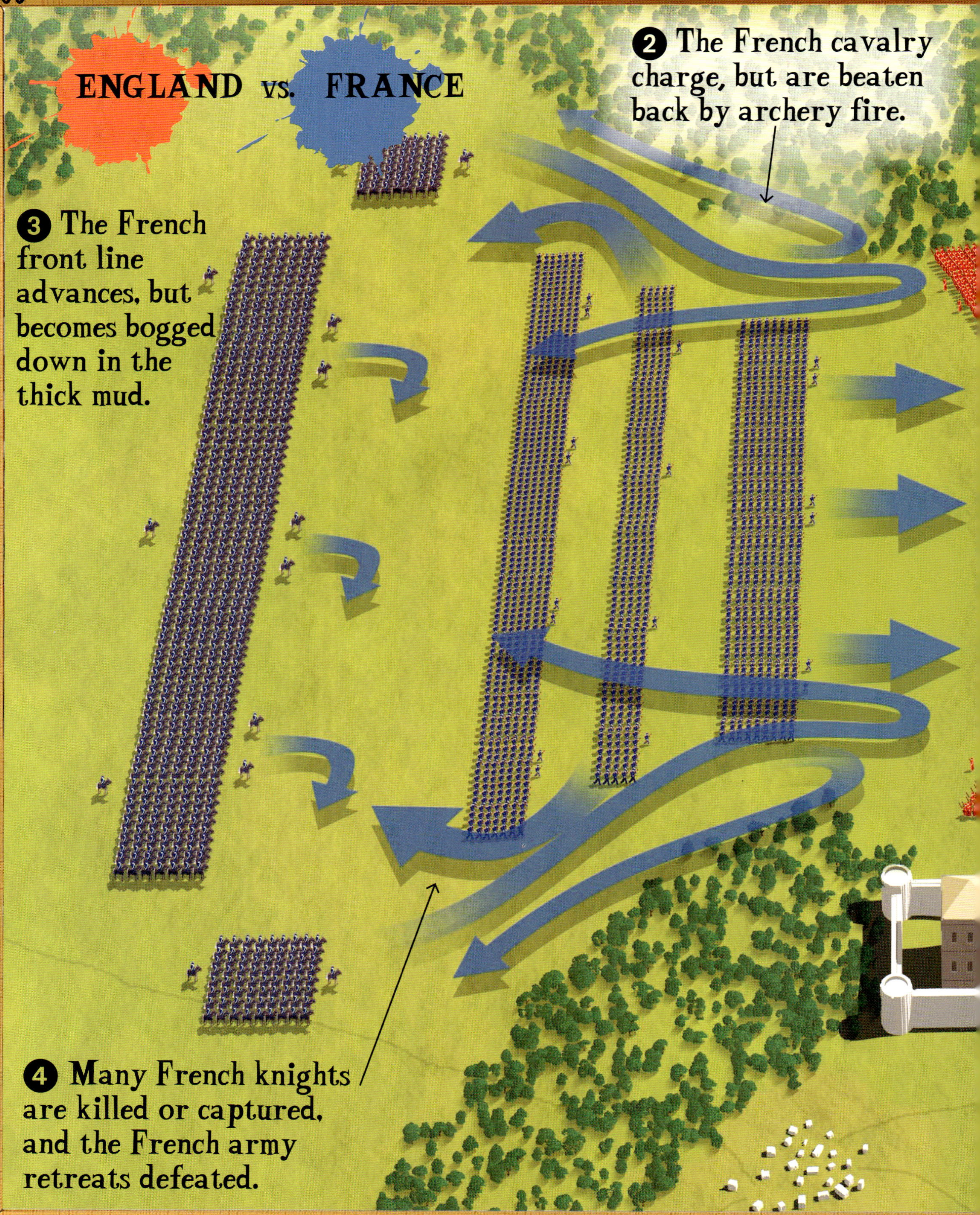
ENGLAND vs. FRANCE
2 The French cavalry charge, but are beaten back by archery fire.
3 The French front line advances, but becomes bogged down in the thick mud.
4 Many French knights are killed or captured, and the French army retreats defeated.

1 King Henry V forms his English troops into a battle line with knights and men-at-arms in the centre and archers on the flanks (sides).
5 A small French force attacks the English camp.
AGINCOURT, FRANCE, 1415

1400s

FIRING A

HANDGONNE

There was an ear-shattering bang and a plume of smoke. By the early 1400s, large cannons were common on Medieval battlefields, but handgonnes (hand cannons) were something new.

Packing a Punch

The simplest handgonnes were little more than handheld cannons, but they fired with such force that they could kill even if amour stopped the missile.

BIG BANG!

Handgonnes were nothing like the matchlocks that developed in the late 1400s. Yet, the handheld cannons were the start of a new form of warfare.

- The earliest were made in China around 1280.
- They were not fast or accurate, but they were easy to use.
- Rocks, nails, iron balls and arrows were used as ammunition.

DID YOU KNOW?

Holding the weapon with both hands, handgonners needed a helper to light the fuse.

Below: Like many Medieval castles, Segovia in Spain was built on a hill, beside a river.

CHAPTER 5

CASTLES AND SIEGE WARFARE

Castles were built to keep enemies out. Capturing a castle could take months while the armies – inside and out – grew hungry and crippled by disease.

Right: A siege cannon could fire 5.4 kg (12-pound) granite balls over 2,000 m (6,600 feet).

BESIEGING

Below: There were many different ways an army could besiege a castle.

A CASTLE

DID YOU KNOW?

It is a myth that crocodiles were placed in moats to make them harder to cross.

Castles were built on hills for a good reason. High ground gave the defenders a huge advantage. Not only could they see an enemy coming for miles, but the enemy would have to climb a hill to attack.

Once up the hill, the enemy faced thick stonework and troops firing missile weapons. Besieging a castle needed cunning and patience.

CASTLE DEFENCES

- Curtain wall: outer wall, up to 6 m (20 feet) thick
- Moat: dry or wet, could slow attacks and make it hard to tunnel under
- Hoardings: wooden platforms built on walls to make it easier to drop things on the enemy
- Towers: lookout posts

TREBUCHET

The walls shook as one tonne of solid stone hit home with a thunderous crack. The trebuchet was reloaded and another missile hurtled towards the castle walls.

DID YOU KNOW?

***Trebuchet* comes from the French word meaning to tumble or fall over.**

Dirty Bombs

Trebuchets were designed to bring down walls. They sometimes threw more gruesome missiles, too. Dead bodies, flung over walls, spread disease and terror.

Above: The counterweight trebuchet worked like a giant lever with a sling.

TREBUCHET VERSUS CATAPULT

- Siege weapons, such as mangonels and onagers, were types of catapults. They worked in the same way as crossbows. They used stored energy to throw missiles.
- Trebuchets did not work the same way. They used gravity to power their attacks.

1187 SIEGE OF JERUSALEM

Time was running out. The army of Saladin, Sultan of Egypt, was waiting outside the walls of Jerusalem. Inside, the streets were packed with terrified refugees who had only just escaped his forces.

All or Nothing!
The people were desperate but determined. They would rather die and destroy the city than see it fall.

Right: Saladin's infantry storm the walls of Jerusalem using ladders and siege towers.

STEP-BY-STEP SIEGE

- Saladin lost many troops trying to break through the gates.
- Saladin changed tactics. Using siege engines he attacked again.
- Undermined walls collapsed.
- With only a few knights remaining, the city surrendered.

DID YOU KNOW?
In Medieval times, the people inside the walls had to surrender or they lost the right to mercy from the invaders.

DEFENDING THE WALLS

Above: Troops could attack while hidden inside a mobile shield called a mantlet.

Castles and walled cities were built for war. Inside their protective stonework, a small force could hold out against a much larger army for as long as the food – and the walls – held.

Nasty Tricks

Arrow loops were slits in the walls. Murder holes were holes in the ceilings. Both were designed so that all sorts of unpleasant things could be dropped on attacking troops.

DID YOU KNOW?

There are reports of stinging insects being released on attacking armies.

DEATH FROM ABOVE

- Hot sand, wax or animal fat: stuck to skin, got inside armour
- Boiling water: scalded
- Burning dung: choked and burned
- Quicklime: caused blindness
- Sulphur: made poisonous fumes

Using ladders to enter a besieged city (called escalading) was risky and daring.

UNDERMINING

In siege warfare, attackers had two options: wait for the enemy to surrender or break through the defences. An attacker who chose the second option had three more choices: go over the wall; go through the wall; or, go under the wall.

Below: Attackers could dig a tunnel, fill it with hay and pig fat, set a fire, and run!

DID YOU KNOW?

Late Medieval castles were built with layers of walls, to make undermining them less effective.

UNDER OR OVER?

Miners and sappers had very different jobs on the battlefield.

- Miners worked below ground, using fire and explosives to weaken the walls.
- Sappers attacked the walls from above ground with picks and explosives.

Above: After undermining, attackers set fires beneath a castle wall to smoke out the defenders.

1203 - 1204

CHATEAU GAILLARD

DID YOU KNOW?
The French used floating towers to protect themselves as they crossed the river below Château Gaillard.

LASTING LAWS

The loss of Château Gaillard was a huge blow to King John of England. Afterwards, King Philip's forces quickly captured the rest of Normandy. John was seen as weak by his own people, and knights were able to force him to agree to a 'great charter' of freedoms called the Magna Carta.

King Philip of France was ready to fight. Since 1066, English kings had been serving as dukes of Normandy. Determined to have Normandy for himself, he attacked the huge fortress of Château Gaillard.

Left: Towering above the surrounding countryside, Château Gaillard seemed unbeatable.

Dig for Victory!

While siege engines did their work, miners were involved in pitch battles as the defenders tried to undermine the attackers' own tunnels.

FRANCE vs. ENGLAND
3 English King John sends relief forces by water, but they are beaten back.
1 Built with its back to the River Seine, the castle could be attacked only by land.
2 In 1203, the French troops dig trenches and build siege engines.

1216 SIEGE OF DOVER CASTLE

After the loss of Château Gaillard, King John of England faced open rebellion. The Barons' War saw the great castle at Dover besieged not once but twice.

UNBROKEN

Miners undermined the outer gateway and brought down the east gate, but they could not break the defenders' spirits. Dover stood strong.

TUNNEL VISION

How could defenders know if an enemy was tunneling under the walls?

- **They could place water-filled vessels on the ground, near the walls.**
- **If the water rippled, then enemy miners were close by.**

CHATEAU GAILLARD, FRANCE, 1203-04

Some battering rams were simple logs carried by soldiers. Others were massive weapons that swung from chains. No two battering rams looked the same, but they all had the same job.

Pounded to Dust

Stone is strong but cracks easily. Rams were designed to pound one spot until the stones crumbled, allowing troops to pour in.

DID YOU KNOW?

Battering rams were used from ancient times to break down walls and smash in doors.

SIMPLE BUT EFFECTIVE

- Most rams were between 4 and 6 metres long (12 and 20 feet in length).
- They were made from hardwoods, such as oak and ash.
- A shelter, called a penthouse, kept the ram safe from attack from above.

Right: Rams could be loaded with firewood and set alight.

DID YOU KNOW?
Dover is England's largest castle. Secret tunnels underneath it helped defend Britain for centuries.

"They mined ... so that one of the towers fell, of which there were two."

(Histoire des Ducs de Normandie et des Rois d'Angleterre, 1220.)

BATTERING RAM

SIEGE CANNON

Black powder – gunpowder – was the terror of the Medieval battlefield. It changed the face of war forever. Armour and swords were little use against guns and cannons.

End of an Era

Two hundred years after black powder weapons first appeared, the world of knights in shining armour and samurai swordsmen had all but vanished.

Above: Attackers used siege towers to bring their cannons closer to the walls.

BOMBARD

An early and simple cannon, the bombard was cast in iron like a bell.

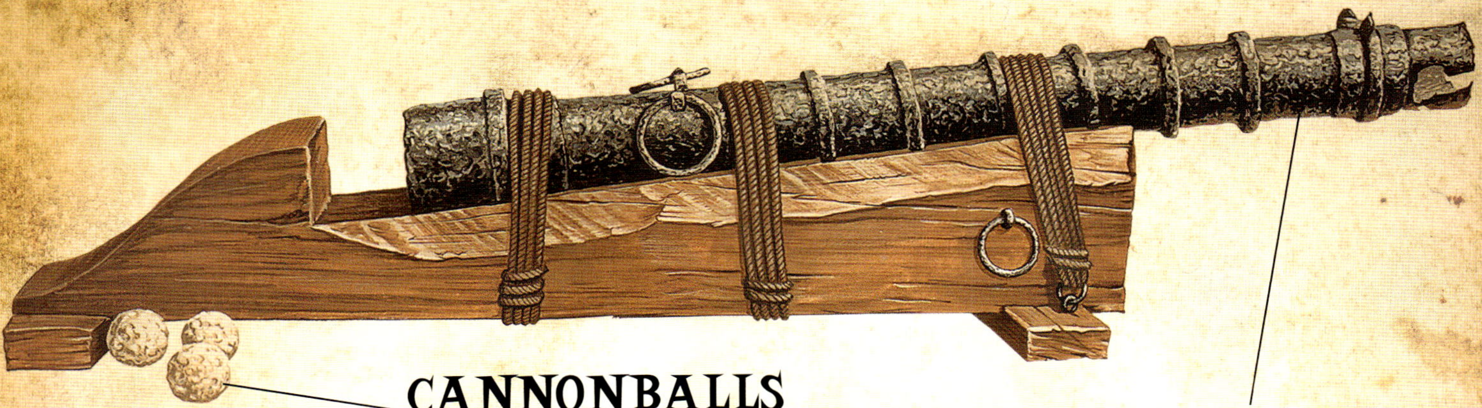

CANNONBALLS
Rounded stone or iron missiles were loaded down the front end of the cannon.

SIEGE CANNON
Longer barrels meant that missiles could be fired further.

DID YOU KNOW?

Cannon **comes from the Latin word** ***canna,*** **which means 'tube'.**

Right: Cannons were tied to wooden frames and platforms so they would not move when fired.

CONSTANTINOPLE

SIEGE FACTS

- The siege of Constantinople lasted seven months.
- The Ottomans bombarded the walls for six weeks before the final assault.
- The attackers numbered 150,000, ten times that of the defending forces.

Below: Turkish cavalry were hit by flaming balls of fire shot by Christian defenders inside the city.

1453

The Roman Empire finally fell on 29 May 1453, to the Ottoman Turkish forces of Sultan Mehmet II. Constantinople had been the eastern heart of the Roman Empire for 1,123 years.

Find a Way, Any Way

During the battle to control the city, a Turk named Orban unleashed a terrifying super weapon. Orban's 'horrifying and extraordinary monster' was a giant bombard, which could destroy entire sections of wall with one shot.

DID YOU KNOW?

The sea route to the city was blocked by a giant chain, so the Ottoman army used greased logs to move ships over land.

GLOSSARY

ammunition – anything that can be fired at an enemy using a sling, bow, cannon or siege weapon

besiege – to surround a city and try to take it over by force

chainmail – armour made of small metal rings linked together

charter – written list of rules

chivalric code – rules of behaviour followed by European knights

equipment – special tools needed for a job, such as being a soldier

flank – the side of something

gauntlet – armoured glove

hacking post – wooden post used to practice sword fighting

hauberk – long shirt made of chainmail

helm – type of helmet that covers the face

heraldry – the design and study of coats-of-arms

Holy Land – land in the Middle East important to Christians, Jews and Muslims, especially the city of Jerusalem

honour – for knights, a term for respect and strength of character

huscarl – a bodyguard in Anglo-Saxon Britain, before the Norman Conquest

kite shield – a Norman shield that was shaped like a kite for protecting the legs when riding a horse

lance – long spear used by cavalry

Medieval – period of history from the 5th to the 15th centuries

men-at-arms – trained soldiers who were armed like knights and rode horses

missile weapons – objects that are thrown, shot or fired

nasal bar – metal strip on a helmet protecting the nose

Normandy – area of northern France settled by Norse people

Norse – a people from northern Europe; often means the same as Viking

plate armour – armour made of plates of metal covering different parts of the body

pole weapons/polearms – where the main fighting part is fitted on the end of a long shaft, like a halberd or pike

recurve bow – bow with ends that curve away from the archer; stores more energy and can fire arrows farther than a straight bow

sagas – legendary tales

scabbard – a sheath for a knife or sword

siege – when an army tries to cut off and capture a city

stirrup – each of a pair of loops for the feet attached to a horse rider's saddle to help the rider balance

surcoat – long, sleeveless outer coat

tactic – plan of action for doing something

Teutonic Knights – German knights who crusaded in Eastern Europe in the 12th and 13th centuries

trebuchet – a siege weapon that used a counterweight to throw missiles

undermining – digging beneath castle walls to weaken them and so allow the attackers to get inside

visor – on a helm, the part that lifts up, allowing the wearer to see

warrior – fighting person or soldier

INDEX